My Writings

The World We Live, Love, and Hate through Poetry

My Writings

The World We Live, Love, and Hate through Poetry

Victor C. Huron

Copyright © 2025 Victor C. Huron. All rights reserved.

No part of this publication may be reproduced, stored in a retrieval system or transmitted in any form or by any means, electronic, mechanical, photocopying, recording or otherwise, without prior permission of Halo Publishing International.

For permission requests, write to the publisher, addressed "Attention: Permissions Coordinator," at the address below.

Images within this book were generated using artificial intelligence technology and may not depict real people or locations.

Halo Publishing International
7550 W IH-10 #800, PMB 2069,
San Antonio, TX 78229

First Edition, April 2025
ISBN: 978-1-63765-777-5
Library of Congress Control Number: 2025905134

Halo Publishing International is a self-publishing company that publishes adult fiction and non-fiction, children's literature, self-help, spiritual, and faith-based books. Do you have a book idea you would like us to consider publishing? Please visit www.halopublishing.com for more information.

Abigail Luna
*Thank you for your insight in helping
me start this book.*

Cynthia Villegas
My Writings *would never have come to fruition
if it were not for that fateful night you asked
me to write a poem for you.*

Contents

Forever Young	12
Time	14
One Life	16
Sometimes	18
Sorry	20
The Sadness	22
Dark Rain	24
Darkened Rain	26
Distasteful Memories	28
Change	30
The Game	32
The Reason	34
Friend	36
Meaning and Purpose	38
Our World, Our Lives	40
Total Control	42
Anima Mundi	44
Getaway	46
Freely	48
Our Eyes	50
Rest	52
Time Restraints	54

Choice	56
Hope and Dreams	58
My Destiny	60
Good and Evil	62
Destruction	64
Spirit of Mankind	66
Troubled Skies	68
Heroes and Villains	70
Elysian Fields	72
Holding Arms	74
Open Arms	76
Firelight	78
Lenses	80
Deals and Promises	82
Pencil and Paper	84
Falling Tears	86
Anger within Me	88
Leave Me Alone	90
Chemically Induced	92
Pills	94
Gatekeeper	96
So Powerful	98
Time for a Change	100
Being	102
Alive	104
Forgotten Memories	106
Hatred	108

My Life	110
Struggle	112
Reins	114
Bringing	116
Today	118
Knocking	120
The Tube	122
Forgotten	124
Heavenly Way	126
Walk	128
Nothing	130
Doesn't Matter	132
So Estranged	134
Win or Lose	136
Unrest	138
Epiphany	140
Acknowledgments	**143**
Let's Connect	**145**

Forever Young

Remember how the world once was
Clear-blue, moonlit light skies
Stars held the dreams that lived forever
Where the young and old could live forever
When the nights seemed to last forever
Living in our minds, Forever Young

Forever we'll imagine a fantasy
A life that takes us far beyond the clouds
Only if the moonlit clouds could last forever
Where we spent deep, thoughtful nights
Sharing a precious moment with a loved one
Living in our minds, Forever Young

Living our lives to fulfill a fruitful, endless song
Wishing we could live forever young
Having the power to dream forever
Enjoying those summer nights, even the cold ones
Where we could dream together forever
Living in our minds, Forever Young

Don't you wish you could live forever
Enjoying every moment with the one you love
Forever in the moonlit skies above
Dreaming of fulfillments yet to come
Staring at the skies above forever
Living in our minds, Forever Young

Time

Time is so invincible
Time is all we have in this world
In time, our story will be told
How much time we have, no one knows

Time can be your friend or foe
A friend when you need someone close
A foe when someone else has control
An imprisonment that ruins and benefits us all

Time revolves on its own
Never told how fast or slow it should go
Time can never be borrowed, only given
We all have a set time in this world

Given at birth and taken in death
Time will send us on our way
Always in our lives, no matter where we go
Time is a never-ending story

Time is everywhere and above everything
Reaching beyond the four corners of the universe
Time was spent yesterday and part of tomorrow
Time, there is only one thing I want to know

Will you let me die of old age, not of a heartache

ONE LIFE

Our lives belong to one another
Pleasant thoughts, distraught ones
No matter where you've gone
We'll continue thinking of you
When the stars shone at night
You helped it shine upon us all

You had your run, you spent your time
Brought smiles, praise when needed
Bless your heart, you won't be forgotten
Now that you're gone from this world
Let our tears cloud all our sorrowed eyes
In the end, we'll have another toast for you

Another starstruck night fills the sky
Your time has come to pass, to be part of time
We'll keep fighting for what we love
We have One Life to live, but we all strive
To make the most of our own lives
We all try to make the best of our time

Now it's your time to join the night sky
Meet the spirit who gave you a joyful life
To start your journey to the heavens
There, you'll go knowing there will be a time
When I'll catch a glimpse of your soul
When it's my time to go

SOMETIMES

Everyone has gone through troubles
Everyone knows how it feels
To be left out in the rain
No one to hear what you have to say
No one to hold you straight
Sometimes you're all alone

You feel deep inside
They turned their back on you
Everyone knows there's a time
You need someone by your side
But there's nobody to fall upon
Sometimes you're all alone

Every now and then
We struggle to be on our own
Feeling cornered at every turn
With only your shadow by your side
The painful lesson learned in life
Sometimes you're all alone

Sometimes we're all alone
Sometimes dealing with it on our own
Sometimes we don't need someone
Sometimes it's best to be left alone
Sometimes it's best to solve it on our own
Sometimes we are better off on our own

Sorry

You're saying Sorry once again
Saying Sorry, an empty feeling
Using Sorry with no meaning
Hearing it once again brings back
Memories of our past times
Arguing about simple things
Looking back and wondering why

I listened for the first, second, or
Even the third, fourth, and fifth time
It led nowhere but a damned end
Why did I give it another run
Knowing it would lead to a dead-end
Causing more pain than deserved
Would have rather just moved on

Yet we're here, once again saying
Sorry, hearing it for the last time
Never wanted it to end this way
But when it must rain, let it rain
Will it finally bring a peaceful end
Where we both can walk away, or
Indulge in another painful storm?

Why can't we just move on
Why can't we just leave one another
Why can't we just hate each other
Why go down this futile endeavor
Why do we have this everlasting lust
Why do we always say Sorry
Why don't we just start all over?

THE SADNESS

Now that you're truly gone
The Sadness has taken hold
Not knowing it would hit me
So Hard, So Strong, So Disheartening
It took me down a lonely road
I've never been down before

It took me long to find someone
Doubting if I can start all over
Whether or Not I should seek another
Who'll bring me back, asking life for more
To refill the empty void left by another
The dark hole the abyss left within me

Is there anyone who can answer me
How to cope with a lost loved one
Who we thought would be the one
An everlasting love, an unwavering loyalty
It took me long to get used to
Knowing you're truly gone forever

Contemplating what lies ahead for me
Feeling forsaken, The Sadness overwhelms me
Now brings out the anger within me
Blaming others, looking for some relief
I just need to wait and see
Believing someone is out there for me

DARK RAIN

I'm the cause of all the trouble
All the pain, and you're not to blame
I guess I never wanted to be
Your True Lover, but just a passing fling
I don't blame you for how you feel
All that I've done now comes down to
A Tragic, Sorrow, Painful, Disdainful End

All the pain I caused due to my own
Selfish, Destructive, Disrespectful Ways
Finally, you had the courage to leave me
Alone in the cold, dark, pouring, lonely rain
Never could I be your lover or a friend
Glad you left me in the cold, dark rain
Betrayed every oath I promised to make

I know there's someone out there
Who deserves to have someone lovely like you
Someone who has true, loving loyalty
I can only wish they don't come from
A cold, dark, pouring, damned lonely rain
That will bring nothing but pain your way
Sorry I caused all the trouble and pain

Darkened Rain

Welcome into my current world
My life until now has been filled
With many Ups and Downs
Living a life leading nowhere
Been down many different roads
Now, I've finally reached the road
That leads to nowhere but a dead-end

My roads have always changed
Causing changes, I never regretted
But lately the roads have led me
Down this dark, lonesome causeway
Where the rain never seems to end
Even the sunlight seems to be afraid
Every turn gives more Darkened Rain

I wonder what's causing all this pain
Done nothing to cause any change
I've led a life with everyday mistakes
It's time to make a drastic change
To put an end to this Darkened Rain
Time to clear my mind, ride the road
That leads me to a place I want to be

Distasteful Memories

Every time I set these eyes upon you
Distasteful Memories reappear
You bring back our past
I left abandoned long ago

I've made many changes
To fulfill this life of mine
They have brought me to this
New place I feel welcomed now

You brought back the pain
That gave me so much disgust
You take me away from this place
A heavenly place I enjoy life now

You took what was dearest to me
Distorted it from what I was
Loyal, Faithful, Trustworthy
You destroyed my inner core

Now as the years have passed
Someone took me in graciously
Dismantling these Distasteful Memories
Bringing me back to what I once was

Eager to take on
What was broken long ago
Cherishing what was wasted on another
Glad I'm valued and loved once again

CHANGE

I've known all my life
One day things will change
For Better or For Worse
If we don't decide to change
It could be the end of things
We all value in our silly, selfish lives
Things that we all seem to be living for

If we just take a step back
And realize what is going on
We'll see how wrong we are
And pray for some revelations
For that's what we all need
Just step back and pray
For we're the ones to blame

We all should cry, just cry
For it's just our own fault
That brought forth this false life
Of useless endeavors
Having no clue what life is for
Let's just say it's time for a Change

We all know it's time for
A damn freaking change
If only we had a truthful heart
We could see down the road
The life we live leads nowhere
All I can say, it's time for us to Change

THE GAME

Another day has me all bogged down
No matter how much I try to avoid
It's something I can't just ignore
Everyone has gone through this before
What brings you up can also be the reason
You end up where you don't want to be
Another song, we all sing along

It doesn't matter how we get through
It's just another bump in the road
Another card from a deck we've chosen
To gamble our lives for we're the ones
Playing the card that has been turned
Betting all against the dealer
Thinking we can outplay the dealer

There will be many wins, but
We must deal with the ones we have lost
For it's what we all experience
No matter how deep our pockets are
We're not guaranteed to win, but only
A chance to play the game we enjoy
Knowing it's our lives that are at stake

The Reason

These cold shivers down my spine
Have always been there by my side
Only one can help in this difficult time
I must look within me and decide how
I'll survive and proceed with my life
I know I've met people who will guide me

When I look into the mirror, I only see
Someone lost in the path called life
No matter how much I try to be free
Hoping for the day the pain will ease
Every day, asking to be left in peace
There they'll be, by my side, guiding me

Holding this inside is like a rare disease
Many say you must learn to let it be
There must be something I love in life
That will take me to that special place
Where my soul can finally be free
For they are the ones who are guiding me

There will always be a time and place
Where you can go and simply relate
To your past for your own future's sake
Thanking loved ones gone and still here
They're the reason why I still love to exist
Guided by ones who truly care for me

Friend

Life has its ups and downs
Down on your luck
Help needed to get back up
Praying to heavens
Looking up at the skies
Hoping for the best
Expecting the worst
Upside down the world has turned

When hope is gone
Drowning in life's journey
Cold shivers as tears fall
Silence overwhelms you
Dreadful thoughts sudden appear
We can't live forever
Life is too short
Everyone must move on

Pride is just a word
Asking a friend for a word
Confiding in a friend
Who offers a helping hand
Compassion outweighs the need
When a friend in need
You'll find a friend indeed

Meaning and Purpose

We're not getting any younger, We're just getting older
I wake up in the morning and look at our world
And wonder what the hell is wrong with us
Looking over our backs to protect what we have
For others will try to take what little we have

Why do you get up in the morning
To work and survive to pay the bills
There's a meaning to our lives
Life is too short to be taken like a short trip
Don't you wanna impact someone's life

What would your legacy be
To be remembered by others respectfully
Or admired by family or friends
Everyone has a meaning and purpose in life
Try to make a mark in someone's life

We know there's more to life
Rather than taking selfies with no meaning
Just to say we were there with no purpose
Don't waste your life with this endeavor
Start placing priorities with meaning and purpose

Don't live just to work and survive
We all know there's more to life
Put away your differences and grievances
Let's all just try to live a life
With Meaning and Purpose

Our World, Our Lives

Why can't we just simply see
What we've done to our world
Living falsehoods, destroying ourselves
Delusional beliefs that have led us all
To decay deeply from the inside
Is there a way to end this disease
That has taken hold of our lives

Should we just let it be, or should we
Move closer to the place we all can one day
Hold one another, allowing us
To reconcile our differences and lead
Our World, Our Lives to a new horizon
Have you ever dreamed of a place
Where we're all welcome with no compromise

Don't you wanna go down the road
That will take us all to a new place
Rejoicing, having a purpose in life
Having our dearest dreams fulfilled
A place where we can live and die
Knowing we will meet people
Who will influence and better our lives

Total Control

There's a darkness in this world
Living among us, within us all
Suppressing all we know is best
Are we gonna watch our world
Fall apart with no return, or put an end
To the depression ruining our lives

If the darkness consumes me
Please be there by my side
If the darkness consumes you
I promise I'll be there for you
If we're both consumed
Will darkness have total control

If we fall for its crooked hand
We'll be destined to have one chance
To undo what darkness has done
We will rely on one another
To solve the problems
Created by no other than ourselves

Will you be there to save me
Will you be the one to help me escape
From this depression that's taken hold
To set my soul free from darkness
That has taken total control
Is there some hope left in my world

ANIMA MUNDI

Once known as a paradise
A place beloved by everyone
A beautiful joyful Never-Never Land
A world full of our own dreams
Venturing to where we please
Enjoying every cool sea breeze

Anima Mundi was truly strong
Until we went too far and beyond
Abusing what was freely given
Taking for granted, for we thought
There'd be an endless fruitful basket
But nothing ever lasts forever

Now look at what we have done
Who would want to live in a world
Being ripped and torn from within
Disrespectful we all have been
Destroying everything in our way
It's about time we start to change

For we are the one deadly disease
Anima Mundi needs some healing
She won't last forever, and we all
Must meet somewhere in the middle
So listen closely, for you'll hear
Anima Mundi crying for our help

Getaway

Believe Me when I say
I need to get away
Far away from here
Anywhere else but here
To any place where I can
Enjoy a cool summer breeze
Have a drink, feel free

Save Me when I say
Take me away from here
Mentally drive far away
To a peaceful getaway
Enjoying life as it should be
Embracing and Enduring
The pains we all face living

Take Me when I say
I need that special place
Where I will finally be able
To be in my own real fantasy
Bringing back the best in me
Oh, I wish someone would simply
Believe Me…Save Me…Take Me…

To my Getaway
Would you like to go
It is a special place like no other
Leaving behind all troubles and heartaches
Simply enjoying our time far away
From the daily pains we all must endure
May our special place be what we're looking for

Freely

We dream of fantasies
Places we can only see
Places we want to be
Special places meant
Just for me, only me
Where I can be free

There's a side of me
Only a few have seen
A side of me that is
Simply very needy
I'll ask pleasantly
Can I please be free

To do as I please
In a place that lets me
Be who I wish to be
A fantasy made for me
A beautiful symphony
Where I can roam freely

Just take me away
To the place I can
Dream Freely, Carelessly
A place of pure serenity
Believe me, it's a place
Everyone wants to be

Just believe me
There's a place
One meant especially for me
Where I can make ever fantasy
Be more than a dream

OUR EYES

Another night comes to an end
A final song, the last dance
Watching the lights shutting down
In a crowded dance hall
Filled to the brim with excitement
Another round, a final call

Another exchange of pleasantries
Your smile brought back memories
As I stared into your eyes
You stared right back at mine
Oh, the look in your eyes is something
I'll never be able to forget

A glimpse into a paradise
A joy shortly to be lived
Simply for my carelessness
Soon after resentment begins
A dark shadow overcomes us all
Across the dance floor

Caught up in the reverie
All the brouhaha separates me
Sorrow entangles, strangles me
A rarity you were to me
I just can't wait to see Our Eyes
Once again glance at tranquility

Rest

I remember when once in my life
I found the one who would take me
To a place I would rest forever
Nothing now can take me away from
The place I've searched, longed for

Never did it occur to me
I would find the one rolling down
A lonesome cul-de-sac without hope
Being nothing more than a dream
That I believed would lead nowhere

When it comes, you'll never expect it
It became clear as the morning dawn
In a river city with a wholesome heart
We may think it's crazy, but we're all
Given a chance to live and love once

Don't say it can never ever happen
For the chance may pass you by
In the blink of an eye and only happen
If you keep a sharp eye for the chance
To find the place you'll rest forever

TIME RESTRAINTS

Remembering when I laid my eyes upon you
In the city with a river in the middle
Living day by day with nothing in sight
Never thought I'd find the only one
Who would utterly transform my life
Changing both of our lives that night

Never thought you would be the one
Who would change my life for good
I never tried to chase you, but it's just
I admire how you made me feel
Knowing I longed to be with you
Wishing I spent more time with you

Even with our time restraints
You still brought light back into my life
Even for a few moments, I'll never forget
So glad I spent precious time with you
Sharing our time together on that lovely night
Changing the course of both of our lives

Now that the years have passed
I stare into those eyes from long ago
As I stand here, I thank the God above
Who brought forth a path for you and me
Our time restraints no longer interfere
Every moment with you is dear to me

Choice

When we die, where do we go
When you die, where would you like to go
With all the places in the universe
Are we able to choose more than one
And venture on an endless road

Whether we like our first or our last choice
Wouldn't you like to visit one more than once
Being stuck in one wouldn't be my choice
Able to visit friends and loved ones
Would surely be our best choice

Many versions of the realms of the afterworld
We cannot be only ones in the universe
Endless worlds, many places we can go
An eternity, would you like to be reborn
Or enjoy the realms at our disposal

Selecting one over another is a hard choice
If you're only able to pick one
May your choice be a worthy one
Whenever we go, let's all rejoice
Whether or not we had a good life
We'll have a great choice

Hope and Dreams

It's a lonely road when you're on your own
No one to turn to, not even the God above
Your heart is broken, a soul torn apart
Crying is nothing more than a whisper of hope
No one is listening to this tarnished soul

Walking the streets, corner to corner
Eating when, what you can
Heartwarming conversations, few and far between
Store windows show a different view
Of what your soul used to be

Laughter has fallen down the drain
Heartfelt dreams, long gone, withered away
Night has fallen for the people
Who live in the grief-filled streets
Looking for a place to get some sleep

Early morning, a nice warm breeze
Food lines for meals to feed the needy
Where the lost can feel at ease
A familiar face with a happy tear
Kind gestures fill the air

Hope and Dreams have reappeared
As we enjoy our morning meal
Rejoicing with company close and dear
Healing our heart and spirit deep within
We all should help a soul when in need

My Destiny

Let me tell you about a dream
I thought it was only a fantasy
Miracles were meant for me
A land where I can roam free
A destiny that's meant for me
Enjoying my life as I please

What a fantasy that would be
My destiny will finally come to me
Can't believe this dream was meant
For hardened dreamers like me
It will bring the best out of me
Would you like to join me

It's not a far-fetched fantasy
A reality that I've been seeking
Come with me to this place
Meant for whoever is with me
Be the one who truly believes
Dreams can be a reality

This dream will be more than just a fantasy
But a reality to be shared with thee
Chasing everything dear to you and me
Oh, how I can dream and dream
Of a fantasy that means a lot to me
I can't wait for you to see this with me

Good and Evil

They say, once there was only darkness
Then the light came upon us
But you cannot have one without the other
Good and Evil have fought since the beginning
And will continue till the end of time

Two sides, one not much different than the other
Their beliefs may be different, but
Their conception was the same in the beginning
Each believes they're the best option
And that the other is damnation

One may cross over to the other and vice versa
Taking what's learned from one
Now combined with the other
Creating something different than Good or Evil
An active choice between Good and Evil

Not taking sides, only staying neutral
Over time the actions by Good and Evil
Cause numbness between the ranks
Ending eons of battles, realizing in the end
They are both one and the same, Good and Evil

Destruction

Destruction lays waste
We are all to blame
Unable to trust one another
It won't be long before
It all comes to an end
And it'll be too late
To swallow our pride

We need to learn
How to hold one another
Or have we turned our back
On each other forever
Betraying our loved ones
Only embracing death for everyone
Destruction will be our fate

Will we ever learn to live together
Or be completely destroyed
Will there be someone
To lead us from despair
Who will carry the burden
Of our own faults and guide us
To finally unite and better us all

Spirit of Mankind

The angel of death is coming
To set the world's spirit free
A judgment set forth by our actions
Punishment for the desecration
We laid upon the world we live in

Unfortunate for the innocent
Who pursued a life of constructiveness
While others pursued a life of self-worth
Casting shame on the spirit of mankind
Leaving the innocent to pay retribution

Sent to assess mankind's moral values
To determine a final verdict
Casting down an unforgiving judgment
Compassion for the innocent
Blatant disregard for the sinful

Dark skies around the world come forth
The sun and moon no longer in view
Only remnants of what mankind used to be
The innocent will remain lords of the world
For penance is the only true virtue

TROUBLED SKIES

I fought for you rigorously, and I've always believed
In all the words you have shared with me
Your faith in me has been so clear
I believe there's more of a purpose for me
My soul belongs not only to me
But to others who are in desperate need

Oh yes, I do believe in what you're trying to achieve
To benefit the ones who take your words and heed
There's a problem, for there are some you're unable to reach
Spreading good faith is good for all to read
I flew around the world and saw many you didn't reach
I saw Troubled Skies globally

I've fallen not because I don't want to believe
I only wish to be here for the ones you left in need
I'll be the one who'll take care of them
I'll try my best to serve you and help guide them
When their time in life comes to an end
I'll try to mend these Troubled Skies laid before them

Heroes and Villains

When all Heroes are vanquished
And Villains rise to the occasion
Darkness is at the edge of victory
One must ask, what is one to do
Bow down and kneel before the unmerciful
Has all honor finally failed
Leaving none other than Villains
To prevail and lead amongst us

Rest assured, death is more valiant
Rather than weeping over fallen comrades
The burden of men is to endure the pain
The greed, the selfishness, distorted views
Of man that have taken hold of us
For we're no more than imprisoned souls
Searching for the Twelve Pearly Gates
To be among the Angels, Heroes, and fellow Kin

Then there are those few who argue
What's the purpose of living…
If everything you love is gone…
And yet, others will rise to the forefront
Unwilling to accept our fate, but
Put it all on the line for the rewards
The risks they'll endure and lives they'll sacrifice
For the chance for us to live proud and free

Elysian Fields

Troubled times around the world
War in places you'll never see
Harrowing screams in agony
Despair spreading, locust feasting
On dreams of our youths' destinies

Sending our youth to fight in wars
Mothers praying in endless tears
Fathers fighting by their sons' sides
Filling the sacred Elysian Fields
With anguished souls and minds

With no regard to lives lost
Sending more to their deaths
Comrades fighting alongside
Hoping they'll stay alive
Or join them in the Elysian Fields

With a rifle in their hands
And a prayer in their mind
With a tear in one eye
And death in the other
Wondering if they're next to die

Every night, the painful memories
Nightmares of a never-ending dream
Of screams, watching comrades die
Joining the Elysian Fields
Hoping for the world to end in peace

Holding Arms

Let's dance to the beat till we fall
The streets are our dance floor
Let's stand tall, holding arms
Marching till our feet bleed
We won't bend at our knees
It's not just a game we play

There's a path we must lead
To show the world we are the ones
Let's stand tall, holding arms
Here to make us all strong
Our words unite us all
Time to make a stand for all

There'll be a time when one will fall
Someone will take their place
Let's stand tall, holding arms
It's worth every bit of pain
Even now, as I start to fall
Will someone take my place

Let the troops stomp and push us away
If you want things to get better
Let's stand tall, holding arms
Fighting for the remnants of the past
When we lived with pride and freedom
Sometimes we must stand ready to fall

Standing Tall, Holding Arms…Together

Open Arms

Let us all drop our firearms
Welcome each other with open arms
Oh, what it would mean to me
To see that beautiful dream
Yet nothing will change if we
Cannot just believe we all can
Overcome and simply live freely

One soul lost to our differences
Is one too many, for every soul
Has something special to bring
To a world that's being torn apart
What's the purpose of living if
We're living just to kill one another
For someone's selfish beliefs

We know this can't continue
We just need to hold each other
In one another's arms and pray for
The moment we can complement
One another and turn this world
Into what it was meant to be
A place for us to live wild and free

FIRELIGHT

As I lie back, looking up
At the blue sky high above
Sighing for one last time
My thoughts run wild
Imagining how the world once was

Sipping on a can of cold Cola
Waiting for the night to end
Letting my love dream away
In our warm, calm bed
Dreaming of how the world once was

Over the horizon, I catch a glimpse
An endless war with one another
Many people around the world
Some like to dream, others are at ease
Let's call for the world to be left in peace

The euphoria once held so dear
Now a delusional drug-filled dream
The skies filled with a deadly disease
Puts an end to our unfulfilled dreams
After the Firelight takes our lives

I believe we'll join a better world
What's left behind, only time will tell
"Learning from our mistakes" may be just a phrase
Let's hope we all can change
What a beautiful world it would be

Lenses

When I look through my Lenses
This is what I see…
A homeless man walking down the street
A single mother struggling to feed her child
A violent crime in front of tear-filled eyes
A world imploding from within

It's not too late to turn it around
Only if you could see through these eyes
As my tears start to fall
We need to retake our oath
To take care of those who are still alive
And respect the ones who are gone

Let's try to make something worthwhile
Try to love one another again
Only if you could see through these eyes
And maybe we would understand
It's not just about our own lives
But how we all belong together

We all have our temptations
What would it cost if we cared for one another
A world where everyone embraced one another
It would be a sight for these tear-filled eyes
Maybe then we all would understand
What these Lenses wish to see one day

Deals and Promises

Everyone eventually is out
On their own in this world
Everyone has something
That needs a cure
Everyone has something
They loved and lost

Keep things you love close
Keep the things that bother you closer
They're the ones who'll take you
For whatever you've got
Remember, every day you must
Put everything on the line

For I made a deal with the devil
How it ends, only I will know
Taking my chances with the choices
The faults and deals I've made
I'll keep my deals and promises
To myself, for no one needs to know

For I made a promise to God
How I keep my word only I will know
My word is worth more than life
When it's time to go, I'll keep my word
I'll keep my deals and promises
To myself, for no one needs to know

Pencil and Paper

Pencil and Paper take me away
To that place where I'll imagine
That my dreams become reality
In a state where I can be
Open-minded and get to write
Explaining how I see the world
Through my own diverse eyes

Romantic for the ones who value
Love and Loyalty above all
For friends who deserve a mention
While I write with my Pencil and Paper
Write to ease the pain of loved ones
Gone from our lives and dearly missed
Or write discreetly about what troubles me

While in this world, I've witnessed others
Causing trouble with no regard to mankind
Self-centered in ways we're all guilty of
Immoral we are at times to the extreme
I've come across a few whom I value the most
Guiding me on this journey as I write
My thoughts about the world I live in

Whatever days I have left, I'll use them wisely
Exploring a gift given to me from above
Having a drink or two, more likely a few
Sharing a toast with whoever is near
Shedding of tears with many cheers
Using my Pencil and Paper as I write freely

FALLING TEARS

Death has come again and
Taken another friend away
Vanished from this world
A journey to a different realm
Into heaven or the nether realm
As the casket closes, who knows

I can feel it again
The anger deep within me
Another set of Falling Tears
A cold feeling overwhelms me
The elderly always say
God works in mysterious ways

I feel the anger
Rise inside me once again
My anger looks towards the sky
My blood-dripping tears open up
And I yell angrily in my head
Why did you take them away!

As I walk through the cemetery
By tombstones with different names
My soul ponders a bit more
Are there angels anymore?
Should I believe in them like before?
What are you waiting for!

Why don't you just take my soul away!

Anger within Me

It was only yesterday
I realized you were finally gone
My heart is blackened
My soul is in total disarray

No reverend could ease my pain
So I turned to the skies
And begged for my death
For now, I roam the earth all alone

Left in darkness in a graveyard
On so-called hallowed ground
My soul starts to scream
You took away!!! What was dear to me!!!

Anguish is all that's left
The painful stricken side of me
Begins to feel the anger within
A forsaken soul is all that's left of me

If I could turn back time, I would
To let you know how I feel
Only if my dream could be conceived
I would greet you in my dreams

Please help me
Help me save my soul
Help me end this anger
Anger within Me

LEAVE ME ALONE

My own shadow hates me
Where I walk, trouble follows me
Leaving destruction behind
I just want to be left alone
I don't want to hear you, or
Want you to share with me
I just want, just want to be
Left alone in my own world

Why won't you leave me alone
I'd rather rot away in my existence
I don't want to hear your message
I just want to be left alone
In this forsaken world that surrounds me
You're causing trouble with the one
Who doesn't give a damn
About this world we all live in

Take your message to that place
Where you can have self-ecstasy
By yourself, leaving me alone
I know you'll try to control me
But in the end, I'll give you
A message you deeply deserve
Just the simple message from me
It's best if you just leave me alone

Chemically Induced

Another night owned by torment
If I could escape, I would go far
Engaged in mind control, I wish
I could just run under the covers
For this is another never-ending
Mind trip that has me cornered

In a world that has me returning
For answers, for questions
Never answered, only postponed
A fate controlled, Chemically Induced
My veins infused with hydrophilic
Tendencies controlled by no other

Ill-wished, brought upon by no other
Who engaged with the unfaithful
Who are nothing but self-centered
Who welcomed the realm of the
Emptiness, Dishonesty, Unloyalty
Oh, please let me start all over

Dependencies or Responsibilities
Whichever comes to fruition
Will lead to the decisions laid before me
Welcome or Not, Make or Break
The choice I'll make, Right or Wrong
Will decide what my fate will be

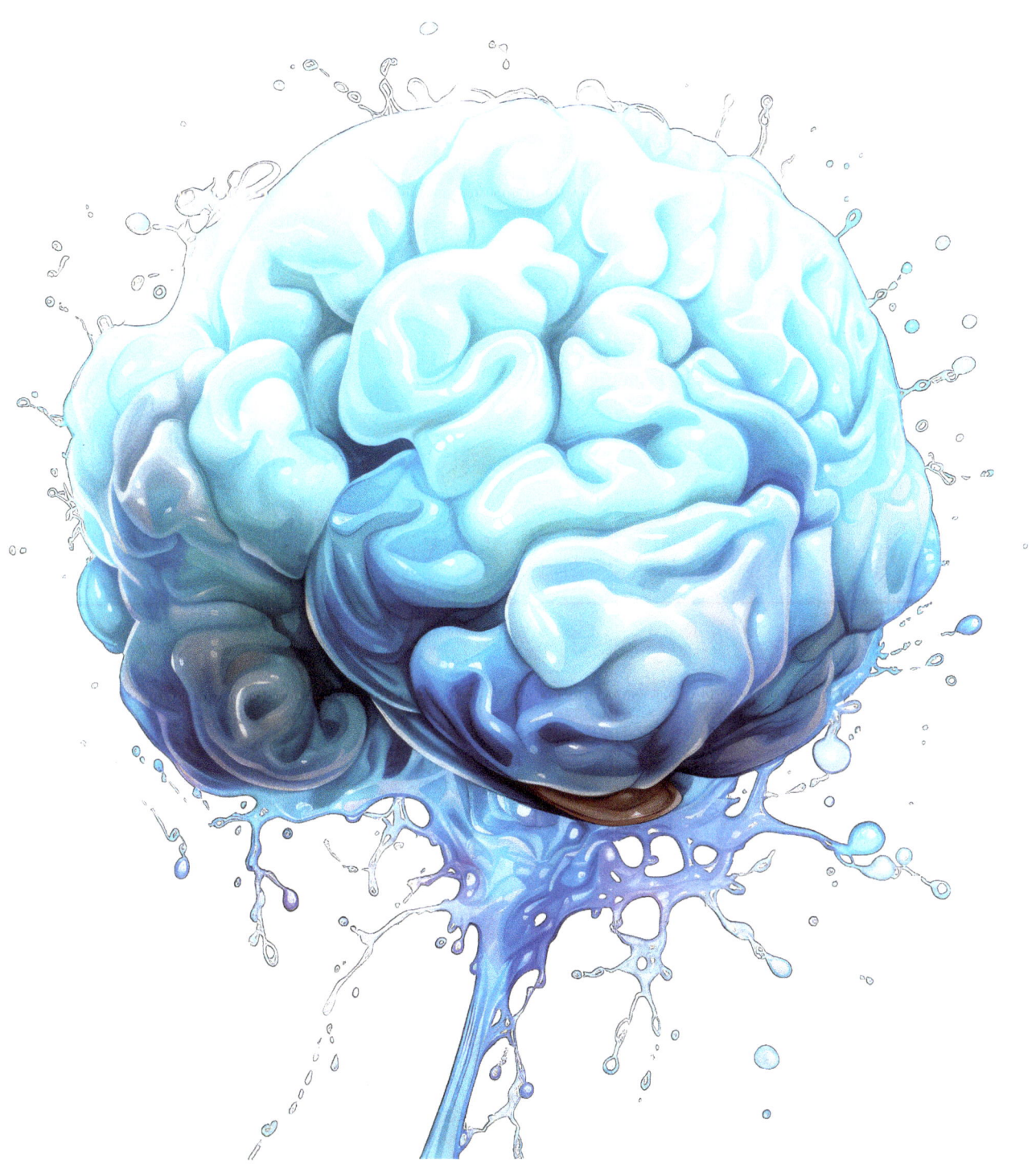

Pills

These pills I take every day
Don't seem to take away
These nightmares that control my fate
Can't seem to make them go away

Can someone help me
Help me take these thoughts away
Will someone make them go away
My life needs to change

Horrible thoughts run through my mind
Of our world coming to an end
Don't want to live anymore
We're so estranged from humanity

Our world needs a cure, for God's sake
Now I hope to see a change
It shouldn't feel so strange
For we are all the same

Or are we going to play this game
The destructive ways we play
Sooner or Later, it'll be too late
We'll all be gone by this destructive game

These pills I take today
Are no more than mankind's
Foolish misinformed messages
That need to come to an end today

GATEKEEPER

When the stress of life implodes around you
Stress can feel as though you're all alone
Inside, you feel that depression has taken hold
Inside your mind, you feel as if you lost control
To the demon who plans to diminish your soul

You tried to break free from this prison
By taking pills to hallucinate
An emotional numbness can't be the way
Accomplishing nothing but sleeping your life away
The demon in your mind never seems to go away

You're dissociated from life, they all seem to say
Escapism is the game you're trying to play
Acting beyond your normal way
The demon in your mind doesn't play this game
Where's the gatekeeper to take the pain away

When will someone come save me
Help me take this pain away
Don't know how long I can live with this pain
I feel there's no other way to end this pain
Where's the gatekeeper to set my soul free

The gatekeeper is none other than me
I must believe I can cure the pain within me
I just need someone to believe in me
I can't fight this demon all alone
I need someone to show the way

God, send someone to help me

So Powerful

A world where one's nightmares
Are another's fulfilled dreams
What we may see one day
May not always be so obvious
A gift to renew one's life given by another
Is so powerful it may never be taken away

One's nightmare consumed by another's dream
Intertwined, destined to meet
One to benefit from the other's need
The needy helping the other to feel complete
We all live in a world with nightmares and dreams
Is so powerful it may never be taken away

A dream once left for dead
Now relives in someone's hands
Reviving another's forgotten dream
Reigniting the fire in one's soul
The hope in one's eyes
Is so powerful it may never be taken away

When was the last time
You gave a helping hand
Taking from oneself
For the welfare of a stranger
Will make a nightmare turn into a dream
Is so powerful it may never be taken away

Time for a Change

We are right here, right now
We need to stop before it's gone
Let's open our eyes
Put our differences aside
It's Time for a Change

We need to agree
To make this go away, or
Witness our own endgame
Things need to change, or
Everything will be gone

Now, it's Time for a Change
Leaving this to chance
It's not something we can bear
Can't be the only one who dreads
Who else fears what's going on

We've got a chance to make a change
Before it's too late
Let's team up and make a change
Leaving this up to chance makes no sense
There's got to be more than war

Right here, right now
We can make it go away
We all know we need to change
We can't live like this anymore
Let's hope we all can change

Being

Being left for dead
By the system we defend
Betrayed by fascist lies
Brainwashed by evil minds
Bestowed only to be given death

Empowering the devil in men
Enduring thoughtless nights
Eager to let others die
Evil resides in me
Evil must subside

I hate how you made me feel
I believed the lies you portrayed
Ignorant to the songs you played
I dread what I've become
I'll never be the same again

Never should have listened
Never should have followed
Never thought about the cost
Now I'm in total disarray
Now it's time to end this pain

Got to mend my mistakes
Got to ask for forgiveness
Got to spend time for healing
God's in the heavens
Give me the strength to be redeemed

ALIVE

Here they are once again
Playing a game, thinking they're gods
Deciding who will stay and who'll be gone
Deciding who are the chosen and who are not
Making friends who are really our foes

Lying to the world about your intentions
Falsehoods from the entitled fools
Who expect to be bestowed absurd rights
When they're no different than the ones they expect
To follow unconditionally with no recourse in return

The promises never meant to be fulfilled
Only to guide the blind to their own demise
Their personal goals valued over the rule of law
The rules of humanity thrown out the door
Sacrificing the many for their foolish goals

Waiting for the one who will put them in place
Guiding the less fortunate and virtuous
Saving the world from their deceiving hands
Rising from the shadows into the light
Men, Women, Children finally open their eyes

Hold their heads high in the new light
Wiping the tears away and screaming that they're Alive
Taking back what was formerly theirs
The crumbling walls imprisoning them are wiped away
Allowing for a new life to begin

Forgotten Memories

As I close my eyes for a moment
Will I see before me what has to change
Humanity is corrupt in many ways
A path of desolation is all that will be left
Indulging in a meaningless mortal existence
Just to end as Forgotten Memories

As I close my eyes for a moment
Will I see before me what we used to be
Or be devoured by our own injustice
As some have foreseen
Falling short of what life could be
Just to end as Forgotten Memories

As I close my eyes for a moment
Will I see before me the river of saddened tears
An ordeal, living through unfulfilled dreams
As time passes before our eyes, are we just living
For the moment, not caring for the unseen
Just to end as Forgotten Memories

When I open my eyes after the moment
Will I see what keeps us further apart,
Or see what holds this world together
We all know nothing lasts forever
I'd rather be a memory of curiosity than
Be part of the Forgotten Memories

HATRED

Watching the world on the tube
How it's become so untuned
Appalled from this small room
Is there anyone left in the world
Who really cares anymore

Has hatred become the norm
Dismantling our inner core
Distorting the truth for the one
Whose morals are less than yours
Can't believe this is happening

Has hatred vanquished all
Has society's ideology changed
Are we willing to lose our morality
Is it too late to refrain
From our foolishness

It's time to leave this hate
I think it's time for change
Or are we hollow inside
There's got to be a better way
To rid the world of this hatred

It's not too late change
Are you willing to devote your time
To leave our hatred behind
I'm hoping to find someone
To help me rid me of my own Hatred

My Life

Let the skies turn dark
Let the stars start to fall
Let the tallest mountains crumble
Let the seas boil and become vapor
Let the world tell you how I feel

I thought you were the one to make me whole
I was hoping I'd found the one
I would finally fall in love
I needed someone to finally escape
I found only tears and pain

Falling short of a dream
Feeling like a discarded soul
Forever pondering what went wrong
Forever to live without the one I love
Feeling lonely, as I used to be

Every day the same nightmare continues on
Every day I hope you come back to save me
Every day my eyes open, looking for a phone call
Every day my life feels as if it will never be the same
Every day my soul and heart yell out your name

My Life feels empty without you

STRUGGLE

Another struggle comes to an end
Trouble taking another breath
My tired eyes are not as crisp
Not as clear as they used to be
During my younger years

I've seen many sunsets
I hope for another sunrise
To get up and spend some time
With the ones whom I'll miss
At the end of my life

My time spent here is not in vain
For I loved all whom I have met
Ones still here and others gone
Who've passed on to the heavens
Now my time has come to an end

I look up towards the sky
And ask if I could have another
Bright sunrise to spend with loved ones
Whom I'll miss the most, for they're the ones
Who'll listen to my final thoughts

Reins

I knew there would be a day
That all would come to an end
The final taste of ice-cold whiskey
Would be my last taste of life
A cold beer on my last night
I would say, "Have a good night."

As I walk out into the cool night
I look back and see the doors close
For the final time, for it's my time
To hang up these old reins of mine
Go home, close these tired eyes
Welcome my final night of life

I've surely enjoyed this life of mine
Seen and felt many sorrows throughout,
This long life filled with many memories
Of loved ones come and gone
As I sleep, I'll dream about joining them
For another rodeo show in heaven

Wishing I had more time to live
But we all must go through our own end
How we accept our own final days
Will help us pass on to the hereafter
As my light begins to fade away
A new sunrise awaits me

BRINGING

I'll take another look again
See if the world has changed
Open these eyes again
Hope I don't hear the same
The world I love is so strange

Now it's time for us to change
Leave behind discontent
Ending rhetoric, we seem to say
All the bullshit we seem to make
Can't be good for anyone's sake

Putting their partisanships away
Ending the prejudices, we all play
Let's try to start a new day
Bring sense to our lives
Try to trust and believe in mankind

The painful bleeding from within
Must come to an end
Bringing hope, bringing love
Let's guard and save our youth
Who must continue living on

Time to open our eyes
Time to end the rhetoric we say
Time to trust and believe
Time to leave something for our youth
Give back what we lost

Bringing Back Hope and Love

Today

Walking in the local park
Feeling the wind blowing by
The stars seem much brighter
More than other nights
As I walk by others
My life comes to mind

Enjoying another night
Listening to music, bringing back
Forgotten, distant memories
Moments that made me
Who I am today
My future is yet to be written

I see children playing
In the same playground
I had the pleasure of playing in
My past youth long gone
Memories of people I once knew
Family, Friends, and All alike

Many are still here
While others moved on to the heavens
Distant, pleasant memories
Walking, enjoying the night
Thinking of those who helped me
Become the person I am Today

KNOCKING

There's someone knocking at my door
I know who it is and what they want
I'm not ready to open my door
I'm not ready to allow them in
My life is not ready to come to an end

They came knocking on my cousin's door
My cousin decided to open the door
He was suffering from cancer in his bones
Overwhelmed with pain, he let them in
In the end, they took my cousin and saved his soul

They came knocking on my two friends' doors
Both enjoying different sunny days
Spending time at the local Canyon Lake
Unfortunately for them, a water swirl took them away
In the end, they took my friends and saved their souls

They came knocking on my parents' door
Cigarettes at the time were the norm
Their hearts full of love became numb
Ceasing to beat due to the thing called nicotine
In the end, they took my parents and saved their souls

No longer young, but not yet old
My health not as strong, but it holds its own
They may come to see if I'll open the door
Be prepared for a fight if you come through my door
In the end, I guess I'll let them take me and save my soul

The Tube

As I watch the news on the tube
I see the world full of death
What's the purpose of life
If we simply wish others death

As I watch the news on the tube
I see mothers holding dead children in their hands
What's the purpose of life
If death is what the young will partake in

As I watch the news on the tube
I see funerals for people who should not be dead
What's the purpose of life
If the less fortunate pay the ultimate in the end

As I watch the news on the tube
I see young women and men in distress
What's the purpose of life
If the young see their future thrown in disarray

When I watch the news on the tube again
I hope to see a change in what lies ahead
There is a purpose in life
To live a long life and live well

Forgotten

Forgive us, for knowing what we have done
Armageddon has come again
Another loss of salvation
All we'll find is desolation
The end of a new generation
Forgotten, their names will be

Will You let the world around us
Fall apart for others' greedy sins
Only to serve their wants and needs
Across the world, people are dying
When there's supposed to be peace
Forgotten, their names will be

You died upon the cross
To forgive us for our sins
The act of love and grace
Would You die for us again
Help us atone for our mistakes
Forgotten, their names will be

The dying young are joining the heavens
Only to be remembered in tears
Our world has fallen from Your grace
Forgive us, for we have sinned
Will You return our humanity, or will
Forgotten, their names be

Heavenly Way

Here comes another night
Frightful in every way
Knowing you're far away
Missing you ever since
You went the Heavenly Way

Help me this lonely night
So I can finally sleep
To join you in my dreams
Help me put my heart at ease
Let me dream you're here with me

My life is like a broken wheel
Throughout the day
You're not here
During the night
I wish you were here

Are you listening? Can you hear me?
Help me end this horrid pain
And I say, "Needed you more than ever!
"You're not gone forever!
"I'll join you some day!"

Wherever I go, I'll think of you
Whatever I'm doing, I'll do it for you
Whenever I need someone, I know you'll be there
I know there will be a day
I'll join you in a Heavenly Way

WALK

At night, I walk alone
I hear the voices
Of friends who are gone
As tears start to fall
I feel the pain
I wish it would go away

At night, I walk alone
Time has taken a toll
My arms are cold
There's emptiness
That's filled this void
Deep within my soul
At night, I walk alone

My mind falls short
The passion of life
Left me long ago
Sorrow takes hold
I feel left alone

At night, I walk home
Close the door
Wipe the tears away
Sleep in my bed
Slowly fade away
Hope it ends the next day

NOTHING

When I took my glasses off
I saw nothing but a blur
I must have meant Nothing at all
Wasted time spent with you
An unfruitful venture I endured
A crumbling bridge leading nowhere

Needing to face the truth
You never were the one
Who would take me to a place
I deeply loved and prayed for
For I long to be with someone
In whom I'll be able to confide

Can't believe what happened
Convicted of the crime of loving
The one who would just simply
Turn off the light, the gem of my life
Left vulnerable in a world
I face alone in the unknown

I guess I should have seen
The bumps in the road before me
A wasted love of a life I gave
Meant for the one who would cherish
What I would give ultimately
Faithfully, Unwavering Loyalty

Doesn't Matter

I'm lost in a world
Surrounded by the deceitful
Fighting over grievances
Which doesn't make sense to me
Is this the end of humanity?

Why can't we just simply behave
Why won't they let us be
I want to live in a world with
No worries, No troubles, No distrust
I'm feeling so distraught

Fighting over different beliefs
Can't they leave our world in peace
Let's put our mind at ease
It's time to shout and speak out
Doesn't Matter what they say

It's time to take back
What they took away
There is only one way
Who else sees it my way
Before it's too late

I am hoping I can find
Others who know what's at stake
Doesn't Matter what they say
Join me to end this game
I know it's not too late

So Estranged

Because of you, I'm so estranged
You destroyed the way I used to live
A false impression of you given to me
The lies you spread about me
That is why I'm so estranged

Because of you I'm in decay
Worsening every day that goes by
My friends even told me to get away
You're like a disease slowly killing me
That is why I'm so estranged

Because of you I'm so angry
Tired of this pain you gave me
You changed me from who I used to be
It's because of you I brought out my rage
This is why I'm so estranged

Because of you I realized
You played a game called make believe
I know what's the best thing for me
To keep the distance between you and me
Now I know why I became so estranged

Go ahead and turn your back on me

Win or Lose

The stars and time must have aligned
I've lived day by day with no end in sight
Till I laid these eyes upon you
Pondering why it took so long
For my life to find the one
Who would be the gift of my lifetime
It's time for me to make that choice

All in on this gambling table
A betting game we all like to play
Win or Lose, we play life's favorite game
Rolling the dice and hoping it lands in our favor
There's no other game we want to play
We'll take our wins and forget about our losses
We will play till we play our deadman's hand

Make your move or lose your turn
This will be the epicenter of your life
It's time to play the lovers' game
Play for keeps, or you'll never know
The only game everyone's eager to play
Be prepared for the lovers' ride
There are many games you'll need to play

Unrest

Here we go, down that road again
Pushing the one we love away
Arguing over senseless reasons
Our love is in constant unrest
Will our love ever be the same
Or do we just like the pain
Is it love or pain we'll leave behind

When caught between the one you love
And the disputes tearing us apart
It's the choice we have to make
It's time for us to change
I don't want to throw love away
I want to go back to that place and time
That brought us together in the first place

If I happened to die today
I would rather be in no other place
Than resting in your arms on that tragic day
I hope we can find love again
Without unrest, leaving the pain far away
Bringing back our love again

It's not too much for us to change

Epiphany

Another night has fallen
As I walk down the avenue
I see streets filled with tears
From souls who've departed reality
I felt an emptiness in my humanity

They once held dreams
No different than you and me
Unable to look away
My curiosity got the best of me
Turned the corner, into the street

I can't explain what I felt
I saw children with parents
With no place to sleep
Cold shivers rose through my veins
Have we fallen so shamefully

Offered a man what little I had
A battered, weathered, but unbroken man
Reached out and shook my hand
Wish I could give more than I had
As I walked back out onto the avenue

The pain in my heart overwhelmed me
Falling to me knees, having an epiphany
Looking towards the sky to embrace
With my heart and a prayer, for I understand
What life is truly for

ACKNOWLEDGMENTS

To all my friends who have known me throughout my life. I've always been there when you needed a helping hand or some advice. Sometimes, in life, we go through hardships, either through faults of our own or because of things beyond our control. Ignoring pride and asking for favors is harder for some than others. Thank you for helping a friend in need, for you're a friend indeed:

Pablo R. Mendoza *Ernesto Victoria*
Jeremy Riley *Ramon Esparza*
James Lee Rivera *Juan R. Ruiz*
Jose A. Ruiz *Victor M. Mendoza*
Joe A. Avila *Juan M. Avila*
Mark Montemayor *Kimy Isaac*
James Combs-Lay *Mark Ramos*

Jose L. Maldonado, Jr.

Let's Connect
Get to know Victor C. Huron

Email: vichuronmywritings@gmail.com

Facebook: Victor Huron

Instagram: @victorhuron

TikTok: @victorhuron

www.ingramcontent.com/pod-product-compliance
Lightning Source LLC
Chambersburg PA
CBHW060950170426
43202CB00026B/3000